Soupline
C•O•O•K•B•O•O•K

Elliott & James
PUBLISHING

<u>Sacred Heart Shelter Mission Statement:</u>

Our mission at Sacred Heart Shelter is to address the barriers to stabilization for homeless families and single women through a continuum of shelter services that focuses on promoting self esteem, dignity, self sufficiency and knowledge in a non-judgmental, communal atmosphere. This is so our clients can begin the process of stabilizing their lives which will eventually lead to their having permanent affordable housing.

Our vision is that through our service, we are planting the seeds of awareness that will enrich our process of growth and that of those we serve and will lead eventually to a just society.

Acknowledgments:

Sacred Heart Shelter is extremely grateful to the restaurant owners and chefs donated the delicious recipes which made this book possible.

ANDALUCA
Bittersweet
Bon Appetit Catering
Donald Collins
Cafe Flora
Barbara Figueroa
Flying Fish
Four Season's Olympic Hotel
Gregg Galuska, Executive Chef and McCormick's Fish House
Garden Party Studio Flowers and Catering
Dottie Haynes
Hi Spot Cafe
Cori Kirkpatrick
Macrina Bakery & Cafe
Marco's Supper Club
Market Cafe at the Westin Hotel
Mayflower Park Hotel
Matt's at the Market
McCormick's Fish House and Bar
Lynn Ove Mortensen
Pirosmani Restaurant
Ponti Seafood Grill
Heidi Rabel
Space Needle Restaurant
Virazon
Westin Hotel

Desk top publishing and cover layout
donated by Shael Anderson 206-283-2130
Original cover art and illustrations by Beverly Davis 206-546-6785

Thank you to these Sacred Heart Shelter Volunteer cooks for thei recipes:

Sharon Finholm
Anne Hickey
Jean Higgins
Michele Hodges
Nancy Moody
Jeff Mills
Sarah Schroer
Gina Ulrich

and we would also to thank the following whose time and generosity made this book possible:

Shael Anderson
Beverly Davis
Helen Horvath
Anita Griffin and the Art Institute of Seattle

Sacred Heart Shelter 1997 Fundraising Advisory Board:

Michelle Audino
Pat Bellamah
Sue Collett
Alex Howard
Gwen Ford
Tom Gillespie
Patrick Kafer
Scooty Kellogg
Karla Kombrink
Nancy Moody
James O'Keefe
Jim Rose

Friend of the Board:

Boyd Sharp, Jr.

King County Executive
RON SIMS

FORWARD

Thank you for purchasing this cookbook and taking part in our efforts to make Seattle a better place to live.

As Seattleites, we know and appreciate our city for what the rest of the country has come to admire. Since 1979, Sacred Heart Shelter has existed to help homeless single women and families find their way back to dignity. It is a place that welcomes those so often forgotten in our community and provides them a safe and supportive haven in which to rebuild their lives.

Sacred Heart Shelter is an integral part of a community effort to close the gap of disparity. To this end, they have compiled this cookbook featuring recipes from some of Seattle's best chefs and bakers, who have contributed their talent to this worthy cause. The enjoyment you receive from the recipes in this book are a testimony to the hard work and dedication of the people of Sacred Heart Shelter.

Your purchase of this cookbook will help Sacred Heart Shelter to continue to provide services and programs to homeless families with young children and single women in our Seattle community.

Thank you.

About Sacred Heart Shelter

Sacred Heart Shelter (SHS) opened its doors for homeless families and single women in 1979. Today, we continue to provide crucial support services to 200 homeless individuals each year. Of these, approximately forty percent are vulnerable children, twelve years old and younger.

Every adult and child residing at SHS has access to clothing, laundry and hygiene facilities, weekly on-site health care, and three healthy meals a day. In contrast to many emergency shelters where a temporary stay may be defined as one night or perhaps a week, residents may stay at SHS for up to ninety days, allowing them more time, opportunity and support to stabilize and explore permanent housing options.

Sacred Heart Shelter provides services and activities to its residents which support them in their efforts towards securing permanent housing and achieving self sufficiency. This is accomplished through the following:

Community Environment:

By providing a fully supportive and holistic community environment, Sacred Heart Shelter is committed to empowering its residents towards self-sufficiency.

Each resident is required to participate in the upkeep of their temporary home, Sacred Heart Shelter, by accomplishing one assigned chore each day. Dinner meals are eaten together to encourage a community relationship between residents. In addition, House meetings are held each week to discuss residents household related concerns, and potential conflicts are mediated by the Direct Service Advocate.

Case Management:

Sacred Heart Shelter assists each resident with establishing and meeting goals by providing both the emotional support and practical assistance necessary to reach these goals. Every adult is assigned to an advocate who helps them facilitate this process. Resources offered by the program include transportation vouchers, access to free childcare, clothing, weekly no-cost physical and mental health care, and referrals to educational opportunities and job-readiness programs.

Transitional Housing:

In 1995, Sacred Heart Shelter, in a unique collaboration with the Association of Apartment Owners of Seattle/King County, established Jump Start, a transitional housing project available to families and single women who have completed a stay at SHS, and who have met the criteria for showing their ability to live independently. By working with an assigned case manager, residents overcome obstacles that may include lack of schooling or job training, confusion about the low-income housing application process, budgeting issues and/or health concerns.

Children's Advocate:

In response to the large number of children residing at Sacred Heart Shelter, a Children's Advocate is employed full-time to access, and respond to, the special needs inherent in homeless children. Every family meets with the Children's Advocate and young children are screened for developmental delays which are commonly found in homeless children.

Obstacles facing these children may include a lack of school enrollment, poor health or nutrition, emotional stress. Often, the remedy can be found in stability and normal playtime. The Children's Advocate arranges for the children to participate in programs such as First Place, a school which specializes in meeting the unique educational needs of children in transition, and Our Place Daycare.

The Children's Advocate also assists parents in increasing their parenting skills through workshops and support group meetings. She may arrange for academic tutoring, and in locating practical items such as kids clothing, diapers, strollers, and more. The Advocate arranges special events, such as parties and field trips and supervises childcare volunteers who come to the Shelter daily to provide the children with extra attention, as well as a positive diversion to the reality homeless children face each day. She also observes for possible child abuse and works closely with Children's Protective Services as determined by state law.

Our services and programs, combined with a caring, community environment helps residents to successfully overcome the obstacles that led them to homelessness.

**For more information about programs, special events or
volunteer opportunities at Sacred Heart Shelter ,
please call us 206-285-7489**

Sacred Heart Shelter is a non-profit agency of the Archdiocesan Housing Authority of Catholic Community Services and is supported by individuals, community groups, the United Way, private foundations, corporations and city,state and federal funds.

Comments from Sacred Heart Shelter Residents:

"I thank God every day that there are still some good, caring people left in this world to help provide for those who really need."

"The acceptance I find here has helped me to be less ashamed of my situation...and the staff has assisted me through the maze of problems associated with homelessness."

"The staff gave me hope that there could be a better future."

Table of Contents

Breads,
Soups
&
Desserts

Northwest Chowder

Ingredients

1	cup onion, diced
1	cup red pepper, diced
1	cup green pepper, diced
1	cup celery, diced
1	tsp. cayenne pepper
1	tsp. paprika
1	tsp. salt
1	tsp. white pepper, ground
1	tsp. thyme, dry
1	tsp. oregano, dry
3	Tbs. bay leaf, ground
1	Tbs. butter
2	Tbs. garlic, minced
6	Tbs. gumbo file
4	cups tomato, diced
3	cups tomato puree
1 1/2	gal lobster stock
1/2	bottle white wine
1	lb. potato, red, skin-on, diced

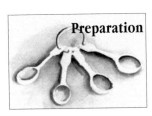

Preparation

Sauté onion, pepper and celery. Add spices, garlic and butter and cook out, scraping bottom of pan. Add tomatoes, stock and wine, reserving 1/2 gallon of lobster stock. Continue scraping to deglaze. Add remaining stock and reduce by 1/3. Add potatoes and cook out. Finish with the following:

> *—Diced fish*
> *—Crab meat*
> *—Bay shrimp*

Fabulous Foccacia Bread

Ingredients

1	pkg. yeast
1/4	cup olive oil
1	cup warm water (100 degree F)
1	lb. flour
	Pinch of salt
1	tsp. fresh chopped rosemary
	Dusting of coarse-grained Kosher salt
	Brush of olive oil

Mix all liquids with yeast in large bowl. Let the mixture sit for 10 minutes. Add the flour, salt and rosemary until dough forms. Knead the dough

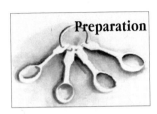

Preparation

for 10 minutes. Let the dough rest for 10 minutes. Roll into a 12" round loaf and push your fingers into the top of the round. Sprinkle with coarse-grained salt. Bake on greased cookie sheet or dusted cornmeal sheet for 15-20 minutes. Brush bread with olive oil straight from the oven.

This bread is delicious by itself, or you can let your creative juices flow with the addition of toppings. After baking, add your toppings and bake for an additional 5 minutes or until cheese melts.

Suggestions:
   *—Sundried tomatoes, artichokes and grated
      Asiago cheese*
   —Blue cheese and caramelized onions
   —Stilton cheese, walnuts and scallions
   —Pesto and Parmesan cheese
   —Kalamata olives (pressed into the dough)

Bailey's Irish Cheese Cake

Ingredients

18	oz. Cream Cheese
5	oz Sugar
4	Eggs
15	oz Sour Cream
1/8	bottle Bailey's Irish Cream

" A crust eaten in peace is better than a banquet partaken in anxiety"

—Aesop

Preparation

Cream the cheese and sugar until smooth. Add eggs slowly, then add sour cream. Add Bailey's Irish Cream. Bake in 8x3 round metal cake pan at 250 degrees F. approximately 1 hour 30 minutes.

Warm Chocolate Banana Bread Pudding *with Warm Liquid Center*

Ingredients

Banana Bread:

8	Tbs. Butter
1/2	cup Brown Sugar
2	Eggs
3	Bananas, mashed
2	cups flour
1	tsp. baking soda
1/2	tsp. Salt

Custard:

2/3	cup Cream
1/2	lb. Bittersweet chocolate
1/2	cup Butter
2 1/3	cup Milk
3	Eggs
2	Yolks
3/4	cup brown sugar

"There is no love sincerer

than the love of food"

-George Bernard Shaw

Banana Bread:

Cream butter and brown sugar until smooth, add eggs one at a time. Add bananas until combined, add flour, baking soda, salt. Bake at 350 degrees for 12 to 15 minutes.

Custard:

Boil milk, cream, add brown sugar, eggs, yolks. Melt butter, add chocolate, milk, add to custard mixture.

Cut banana bread in cubes. Soak with custard filling, Press bread in 3" ring about 2/3 high, add small amount of ganache* in middle (cover with more bread). Bake for 15 minutes at 350 degrees in a one pound loaf pan.

*ganache is a chocolate cream which can be purchased in the gourmet food section or food specialty stores.

Peach Pie

Ingredients

By Victoria Binuya

Makes one 9-inch pie.

Filling:

2 1/2	lb. peaches, washed, pitted and sliced
1/3	cup all-purpose flour
1/2	cup granulated sugar
1/2	tsp. cinnamon
1/4	tsp. nutmeg
1/8	tsp. ground ginger
1	Grated peel and juice of lime
3	Tbs. butter, cut into pieces

Crust:

2 1/2	cups all-purpose flour
1 1/2	Tbs sugar
1	tsp. salt
1	cup cold butter, cut into pieces
1/4 -1/2	cup ice water

Topping:

2	tsp. milk
2	Tbs. brown sugar
1	tsp. flour
1/4	tsp. cinnamon

Preparation

Filling:

Put the peaches in a bowl and toss with flour, sugar, cinnamon, nutmeg, ginger, lime peel and juice. Set aside while preparing the crust.

Crust:

Put flour, sugar and salt in a food processor. Add pieces of butter, and process a few seconds to attain a coarse texture only. With the processor running, add only enough ice water through the feed tube so that the dough holds together. Roll out crust to 1/8-inch thickness, and allow crust to overhang a 9-inch pie pan about 4 inches.

Put the filling into the pastry-lined pan, and dot with 3 tbs. butter. Fold crust overhang up over the fruit, gather into the center and twist into a decorative bun.

Topping:

Brush the crust with milk. Combine the brown sugar, flour and cinnamon. Sprinkle over the top of the pie. Place on a baking sheet and bake in a preheated 400-degree oven for 30 minutes. Turn heat to 350 degrees and continue baking 20 more minutes.

Serve warm with a scoop of vanilla ice cream.

11

Ginger Orange Creme Brulee

Ingredients

3   cups heavy cream
         Grated ginger root
7   egg yolks
2/3   cups sugar
         Pinch of salt

Heat to just under a boil, 3 cups heavy cream and grated ginger root. Combine 7 egg yolks, 2/3 cups sugar and pinch of salt.

Preparation

Combine the cream with the egg mixture. Strain. Add the zest of two oranges and pour into ramekins*. Bake in a water bath in a 350 degree oven until the custard takes on a Jello-like appearance when slightly shaken. Wrap with plastic and chill. Dust the cover with dried brown sugar and torch to broil for serving. Optional: Garnish with two biscotti and crystallized ginger

*a ramekin is a small, individual baking dish

13

Breakfast Bread Pudding with Fruit Compote

Ingredients

Serves 4

Bread Pudding:
8	cups Day-old bread cubes (approx. 1" x 1")
2	Tbs. Butter, melted
4	cups Milk
1	cup Half & Half
3/4-1	cup Honey
1	tsp. Cinnamon
3	Yolks
2	Whole eggs

Fruit Compote:
1	cup Fresh blueberries
1	cup Raspberries
1	cup Fresh strawberries
3/4	cup Sugar
1	Tbs. Flour
1/4	tsp. Cinnamon

14

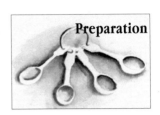

Preparation

Bread Pudding:

Combine milk, half & half, honey, eggs and spice. Toss the bread crumbs in the melted butter and place in a buttered ceramic baking dish. Pour milk mixture over cubes and dunk bobbing cubes. Top with chopped nuts or oats and a light sprinkling of brown sugar. Cover with foil and place in a water bath to bake for 45 minutes at 325 degrees; then remove foil and finish for another 15-20 minutes. Check center for solid, not liquid-like, center. Depending on the depth of the baking dish, it will take longer if 4-5" high. The recipe is designed for a 2-3" dish.

Fruit Compote:

Combine sugar, flour and cinnamon. Toss with blueberries and raspberries. Bring mixture to a boil and taste for sweetness and consistency. May need to add extra sugar or lemon to balance flavor. Add quartered strawberries to warm compote. Serve warm over bread pudding.

15

Space Needle Apple Pie

Ingredients

by Chef LeMaster
& Sous Chef Dry

Apple Pie Filling:

1	each pre-made 8" pie crust
2	Granny Smith apples
2	Red Rome apples
1/4	cup All-purpose flour
1/2	cup Granulated sugar
1	tsp. Cinnamon, ground
1/8	tsp. Nutmeg, ground
1/8	cup Lemon juice
1/2	tsp. Vanilla extract

Apple Pie Topping:

1 1/2	cups Brown sugar
1 1/2	cups All-purpose flour
1 1/2	cups Walnuts, chopped coarse
1	cup Whole unsalted butter, room temperature

Apple Cinnamon Caramel Sauce:

4	cups Apple juice
1	oz.(1/4 cup) Dried apples, minced
1 1/2	cups Whole unsalted butter
2	pinches Cinnamon, ground

Apple Pie Filling

Peel apples, core and slice 1/4 inch thick. Add the vanilla extract and lemon juice to the apples and toss well. In a separate container, mix all dry ingredients well. Add dry ingre-

dients to the apple pie mixture and toss well. Place the pie filling into the pie crust and cover with the topping. Bake at 275 degrees F for 1 hour.

Apple Pie Topping

Soften butter in mixer at low speed for 3 minutes. In a separate container, mix all dry ingredients well. Gently mix all dry ingredients into softened butter. Set aside.

Apple Cinnamon Caramel Sauce

In a stainless steel sauce pan, combine the apple juice and minced dried apples. Cook the mixture on high heat until it's the consistency of a light syrup. It should take approximately 20 minutes. Remove the pan from the heat and slowly add the whole unsalted butter. It is best to add the butter in small amounts while gradually stirring. Repeat the procedure until all of the butter has been blended into the mixture. Add the cinnamon to taste.

> NOTE: This mixture is very sensitive to heat. Avoid exposing to excessively cold or high temperature.

Presentation:

Cut the apple pie into 6ths. Warm in an oven at 200 degrees for approximately 10 minutes. Remove a slice of pie and place on a plate. Drizzle the apple cinnamon caramel glaze liberally over the top. Optional: Garnish with dried cranberries and fresh mint.

17

Walnut Tart

Ingredients

Pastry Chef: Robin Reiels

Makes one 9" tart

Crust:

12	oz. unsalted butter, softened
1	cup powdered sugar
	pinch of salt
3	cups flour

Filling:

1/3	cup honey
2/3	cup sugar
1	cup brown sugar
1/3	cup (3 oz.) unsalted butter
1/4	tsp. salt
4	cups walnuts
3/4	cups heavy cream.

"It's good food and not fine words
that keep me alive"

—Moliere

18

Preparation

Crust:

Beat butter until light and fluffy. Add sugar and salt, mix together well. Slowly add flour until well combined. Press dough into a greased 9" tart shell. Bake at 350 degrees until golden brown, about 20 minutes.

Filling:

In a saucepan over medium heat, stir together honey, sugar, brown sugar, butter and salt. Bring to a boil and cook for 4 minutes. Remove from heat and stir in nuts and cream. Cool for 10 minutes, then spoon into shell. Refrigerate until firm. Serve at room temperature.

Any Morning Muffins

Ingredients

by Michele Hodges,

Makes about 24 muffins
Preheat oven to 400 degrees

Combine:

2	cups buttermilk
1/2	cup honey
3	eggs
2	cups brown sugar
1/2	cup melted butter

Mix until well dissolved.

Stir together dry ingredients:

3	cups flour
3	cups bran
1	tsp. salt
1/2	Tbs. baking soda
1/2	tsp. cinnamon

Preparation

Add liquid mixture all at once and stir until just moist. Don't stir much. Gently fold in 1 cup of either fresh blueberries or fresh cranberries. Spoon into paper-lined muffin pans to 3/4 full. Bake 20-25 minutes at 400 degrees.

Sweet Potato Soup

Ingredients

Serves 4 to 6

1 or 2	(12 oz) Sweet potatoes
1	qt. Chicken stock
1/2	cup Heavy cream
1/2	cup Swiss cheese, grated
	Salt
	Freshly ground pepper

Preparation

Preheat oven to 350 degrees. Wash the potatoes and dry them. Place potatoes on a baking sheet and bake for 1 to 1 1/2 hours or until very soft.

When they are cool enough to handle, peel the potatoes. Blend them with some of the stock, or puree them with a food mill until very smooth. Blend in the rest of the stock and heavy cream. Place the soup into a pan over low heat. When hot, add 1 teaspoon salt and 1/2 teaspoon pepper.

Just before serving, whisk the grated cheese into the hot soup and stir until it melts. Don't cook the soup too long after you have added the cheese, or the cheese will become stringy. Taste for seasoning, and adjust if necessary.

"Give me some repast,

I care not what,

so it be wholesome food"

- William Shakespeare,
Taming of the Shrew

Minestrone, Milanese Style

Yield: 8 to 10 servings.

Ingredients

2	oz. Rice
2	qt. Beef broth
3	oz. Pancetta, chopped
1	fluid oz. Olive oil
2	oz. Onions, diced small
2	oz. Carrots, diced small
2	oz. Celery, diced small
6	cloves Garlic, minced
3	oz. Fresh cranberry beans, shelled
2	oz. Savoy cabbage, cut in squares
2	oz. Potatoes, diced small
4	oz. Tomatoes, peeled, seeded and diced
2	oz. Zucchini, diced small
2	Tbs. Parsley, chopped
1	Tbs. Sage, chopped
1	Tbs. Basil, chopped
	Salt and freshly ground black pepper—To taste
	Nutmeg—To taste

Garnish:

1/2	cup Precooked Green Peas (cooked, shocked in ice water and kept cold for good color)
1/2	cup Grated Parmesan
1/4	cup Extra-Virgin Olive Oil
8-10	Basil Leaves

24

Preparation

Cook the rice, covered, in the beef broth for about 18 minutes. Drain off the broth, and reserve broth. Place the cooked rice in a small container mixed with a little olive oil.

Render the pancetta in the olive oil. Add the onions, carrots, celery and garlic, and cook over medium heat. Add the reserved beef broth and simmer for a few minutes before adding the shelled cranberry beans, cabbage and potatoes. Continue simmering for 6 to 8 minutes. Add the diced tomatoes, zucchini and chopped herbs, and cook for another 5 minutes.

Add salt, pepper and nutmeg. Add the rice.

Serve in soup bowls or cups garnished with the green peas, grated parmesan, and extra-virgin olive oil. Decorate immediately before serving with a fresh basil leaf.

25

Puget Sound Clam Chowder

Ingredients

Makes one gallon.

1	cup Diced celery heart
1	cup Diced yellow onion
1	cup Diced and peeled red potato
2	oz. Diced smoked bacon
1	qt. Clam nectar (not juice)
1	qt. Whole baby clams (shucked)
4 1/2	oz. Flour
4	oz. Butter
1/4	tsp. Fresh thyme
1	tsp. Crushed black pepper
1-2	Bay leaves
1	tsp. Garlic, minced
	White pepper
	Salt

"Man cannot live
by bread alone"

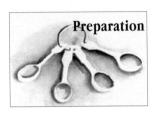

Preparation

Sauté bacon in large, heavy-bottom pan until lightly brown. Remove bacon. Add butter to bacon fat, and sauté onions until tender. Add celery and sauté for 2 minutes. Add flour and stir well, making a roux with the butter. Add clam nectar, stirring well until thick and smooth. Add potatoes and cook slowly for 15-20 minutes. Stir occasionally. Add clams toward the end. Finish with 1 cup hot cream.

Butternut Squash Soup

Chef Astolfo Rueda

Ingredients

3 1/3	qt. Vegetable stock
2	sticks Celery, finely diced
1	Large onion
5	Shallots, finely diced
3	Medium carrots, finely diced
2	cloves Garlic, finely diced
2	Bay leaves
1	bunch Thyme, finely chopped
2	Butternut squash, medium size
3 2/3	Tbs. Pure hazelnut oil
1	Cinnamon stick
	Salt and pepper—to taste

*"A hungry stomach
is not a good political advisor."*

—Albert Einstein

28

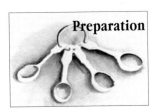

Preparation

*Cut and seed the squash
and place them in a roasting
pan. Add salt, pepper and oil.
Cover the roasting pan with
aluminum foil, and cook in a
medium oven (350 degrees) until fork tender.*

*In the meantime, sweat the vegetables with 1 table-
spoon of oil. Add the garlic, bay leaves and thyme.
Mix everything together, add the stock, bring to a boil,
and let simmer for 30 minutes. Once the squash is
ready, take it out of the shell and puree it in a food
processor, adding the strained broth little by little until
a nice, smooth texture is achieved. Warm up the soup,
adding salt and pepper.*

Northwest Seafood Chowder

Ingredients

2	slices 1/4" Diced raw bacon
1	cup 1/4" Diced onion
1/2	cup 1/4" Diced celery
1	Bay leaf
1	tsp. Dried thyme
1/4	cup All-purpose flour
2	cups Clam juice
2	cups Whole milk
2	each 1/4" Diced Russet potatoes
2	cups Minced clams
1	cup Heavy whipping cream
6	oz. Bay scallops
6	oz. Salmon, deboned
6	oz. Halibut, deboned
	Tabasco®—to taste
	Salt and pepper—to taste

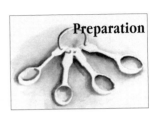

Preparation

In a 2-quart pot, cook bacon over medium heat. Add onion, celery, thyme, bay leaf, potatoes, salt and pepper, and saute until celery is transparent. Add flour and cook on low heat for 3 minutes. Add clam juice, minced clams, halibut, scallops and salmon. Simmer for 10 minutes on low heat. Heat milk and cream to just below boiling point. Add milk and cream to seafood. DO NOT BOIL. Adjust seasoning with salt, pepper and Tabasco®. Garnish with fresh chopped parsley.

Rock Shrimp Corn Chowder

Ingredients

Chef Matt Janke

Makes about 3 quarts.

1	large red onion, finely chopped
2/3	cup flour
1	cup olive oil
7-8	cups hot chicken stock
4	ears of corn, kernels cut from the cob
1 1/2	lb. red potatoes, diced
1 1/2	lb. fresh rock shrimp
1	cup cream
1	cup milk
1/2	bunch fresh basil, chopped
	Salt and pepper—to taste

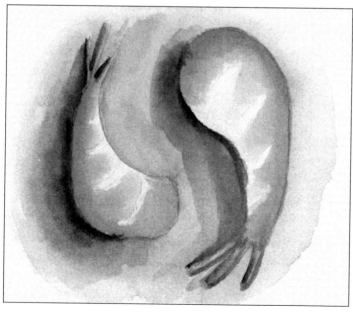

Preparation

In a large, heavy-bottomed sauce pan, sauté onion in 4 tablespoons of oil over medium high heat until onion begins to turn brown.

Add remaining oil and flour. Cook for 5 minutes, mixing completely.

Add chicken stock. Whisk together until smooth.

Add corn and potatoes. Lower heat to medium, and simmer until the potatoes are just tender.

Add rock shrimp, cream and milk. (If fresh rock shrimp are not available, chopped peeled prawns may be substituted.) Simmer until shrimp are cooked. DO NOT ALLOW TO BOIL.

Add basil. Season to taste with salt and pepper.

Roasted Root Vegetable Soup

Ingredients

Yield 12 cups.

1	Yam
2	Carrots
2	Beets
2	Potatoes
3	Tomatoes
2	Stalks celery
1	Red bell pepper
1	Small onion, diced
4	Cloves garlic, chopped
12	Cups vegetable stock or broth
1	tsp. Oregano
1	tsp. Parsley
1	tsp. Thyme
1	tsp. Caraway
1	Tbs. Salt
1	Tbs. Pepper

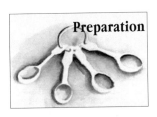

Preparation

Cut yam, carrot, beets, potato and tomato in a large dice of the same size. Small-dice the celery, bell pepper and onion. Toss the yam, carrot and beet in 1 tbs.. olive oil, a big pinch of salt, pepper, garlic, and the dry herbs. Roast at 400 degrees until soft, but firm.

Saute the celery, onion and red pepper with the remaining garlic until onion and pepper are soft. Add the vegetable stock and the diced potatoes. Cook until potatoes are tender, add the roasted vegetables and diced tomatoes. Cook for 15 minutes and taste for seasonings.

Double Garlic Soup

Ingredients

(For a very large group)

Yield: 56 Portions

6	lb. peeled garlic cloves
2	gal.+ 1 qt. Chicken stock
2	Tbs. thyme, chopped
8	bay leaves
1	qt. + 1/2 cup Half and half
1 1/2	cups Madeira
1 1/2	cups Grated Parmigiano Reggiano cheese
1 1/3	lb. Elephant garlic cloves, peeled
3	oz. (1/2 Tbs.. per portion) Chive oil (made by infusing olive oil with chives and straining out solids)
1	generous cup (1 tsp. per portion) Chives, finely minced

Preparation

Combine peeled garlic, chicken stock, thyme and bay leaves in a large pot. Simmer until garlic is tender (about 1/2 hour), stirring occasionally.

Add half and half, Madeira and cheese. Heat through.

Puree mixture in blender or food processor until smooth. Strain through fine mesh strainer. Season with salt and pepper. Keep warm.

Cook elephant garlic by covering with salted water in a saucepan, bringing to a boil, simmering for about 5 minutes, and draining. Repeat the process until garlic is tender. Chill. Cut across in thin slices.

To serve, ladle 6 oz. of the soup into a heated bowl. Float elephant garlic slices on top. Garnish with chive oil (using a squeeze bottle to make a pattern) and minced chives.

Chive Flower Muffins

Ingredients

5	oz. Pastry Flour
5	oz. All-purpose Flour
1/2	tsp. Baking Powder
1/2	tsp. Clarified Butter
4	oz. Buttermilk
1/4	oz. Salt
2	tsp. Chives (diced)
1	tsp. Onions (diced)
24	pieces Chive Flowers
4	oz. Soft Butter

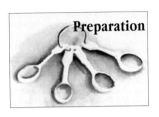

Mix all dry ingredients together. Add the buttermilk, butter, chives and onions. Mix well. Divide the dough into 24 portions into small greased muffin tins. Place a chive flower on each and then a small piece of soft butter on each. Bake in a preheated oven at 375 degrees for 8 to 10 minutes.
Serve warm.

*To clarify butter: Melt butter in a pitcher. Let it settle; remove the fat.

"A diet of food gives us bodily health,
a diet of people
gives us tranquility of the soul"

—Bernadin de St. Pierre

Whole Roast Chicken Soup

Ingredients

***Compliments of
Executive Chef Sear***

Roasted Chicken:

1	2 1/2 lb. Grain-fed chicken
1	tsp. Fennel seeds.
1	tsp. Mustard seed (crushed)
1/2	tsp. Chili flakes
2	tsp. Chopped parsley
2	tsp. Chopped garlic
1	tsp. Black pepper (cracked)
2	tsp. Chopped ginger

Olive oil

Vegetables:

1/2	lb. Pearl onions
1/2	lb. Baby carrots
1/2	lb. Parsnips (peeled and cut lengthwise)
6	cloves Garlic
1/2	lb. Baby turnips
	Salt to taste
3	bottles Evian Water
1	bottle Sparkling mineral water
3	oz. Butter

40

Roasted Chicken:

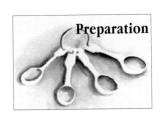

Preparation

Mix all the ingredients together and rub into the chicken cavity and under the skin of the bird. Let stand overnight. Roast in a preheated oven at 450 degrees for 15 minutes.

Vegetables:

Sauté the vegetables in the butter and place into a large stock pot. Add chicken and cover with the water. Bring to a boil and remove any foam from the top. Simmer for 1 1/2 hours. Remove the chicken, and cut away the meat from the bone. Place the meat in preheated bowls. Add vegetables and top off with the hot stock. Sprinkle with chopped Italian parsley.

41

Tomato Bread Soup

Ingredients

Yield: 16 1/2 cups

2	cups Onion, diced 1/4"
1/4	cup Olive oil
1	Bay leaf
1	tsp. Thyme, fresh, minced
3	Tbs. Sugar
2	tsp. Salt mix 3:1
1	Tbs. Paprika(Spanish-sweet)
1	#10 can Tomatoes, whole, in juice
1/2	tsp. Black pepper, fresh ground
4	cups Potato bread, diced in 1/2" cubes
4	cups Water, cool
1/4	cup Red wine
2	tsp. Garlic, fresh, minced

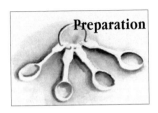

Preparation

In large soup pot, sauté onions in olive oil until translucent and pale golden brown. Add remaining ingredients and slowly bring to boil, stirring occasionally. When it boils, turn down to low heat and simmer for 15 minutes, puree in food processor until smooth.

Vegetable Soup

Submitted by Sarah Schroer

Ingredients

1/4	cup Barley
4	Potatoes, cubed
3	Carrots, sliced
1	can Cut tomatoes
1	Small onion, chopped
3/4	cubes Beef flavoring (vegan option: 3 pkgs. George Washington broth)
1	Tbs. Oil
1/4	Cabbage, chopped
2	Small Zucchini, halved and chopped
1	can Kidney beans
3/4	cup Small pasta shells
1	pkg. Frozen cut green beans
	Dried parsley flakes
	Salt—to taste

Preparation

Place barley, potatoes and carrots in large kettle, half full of cold water. Bring to a boil. Reduce heat to medium high. Add canned tomatoes, onion, seasoning and oil. Cook for 25 minutes. Add cabbage, zucchini, beans, pasta shells and green beans. Cook for 20 more minutes. Sprinkle parsley flakes on top. Salt to taste.

This recipe can be adjusted in size. Add more water and vegetables until desired amount.

Nanaimo Bars

Ingredients

Submitted by Sharon Finholm

Bottom Layer:

1/2	cup butter
1/4 c	up granulated sugar
5	Tbs. cocoa powder
1	egg, beaten
1 3/4	cups graham-cracker crumbs
1	cup coconut flakes
1/2	cup finely chopped walnuts

Middle Layer:

1/2	cup salted butter
3	Tbs. whipping cream
2	Tbs. vanilla pudding mix

(uncooked, NOT the instant variety)

2	cups powdered sugar

Top Layer:

4	squares (1 oz. ea.) semi-sweet chocolate
2	Tbs. butter

"*Happiness is made by the stomach*"

—*Voltaire*

Bottom Layer:

Melt butter, granulated sugar and cocoa powder together in the top of a double boiler over simmering water.

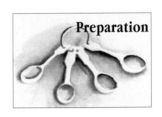

Preparation

Add the egg and stir constantly until thickened, approximately 2 to 3 minutes. Remove from heat. Stir in graham cracker crumbs, coconut and walnuts. Press firmly into an ungreased 8x8-inch pan. Chill.

Middle Layer:

Cream butter, whipping cream, vanilla pudding and powdered sugar together. Beat until light. Spread over bottom layer. Chill

Top Layer:

Melt chocolate and butter over low heat. Cool. When cool, but still liquid, pour over second layer and chill in refrigerator about 15 minutes. Cut into bars. (These bars can be made 3 to 4 days ahead and kept covered and refrigerated).

Apple Crisp

Ingredients

6	cooking apples (approx.)
1	cup sugar
1	cup graham cracker crumbs
1/2	cup flour
1/2	cup chopped walnuts
1/2	tsp. cinnamon
1/8	tsp. salt
1/2	cup (1/4 lb.) butter

"Hope is a good breakfast,
but it is a bad supper"

—Francis Bacon

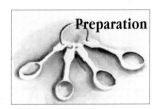

Slice apples and place in pan. Combine dry ingredients. Cut in butter until crumbly. Lightly pack mixture on top of apple slices. Bake at 350 degrees for 1 hour or until apples are tender. Serve with lightly sweetened whipped cream.

Coconut Joys

Submitted by Jean Higgins

Ingredients

Makes about 30

1/2	cup butter or margarine
2	cups powdered sugar
3	cups (8 oz.) shredded coconut
6	oz. pkg. chocolate chips, melted

"We may live without poetry,
music and art;
We may live without conscience
and live without heart;
We may live without friends,
we may live without books;
But civilized man cannot live
without cooks.!!"

—E. R. Bulwer-Lytton

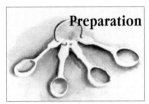
Preparation

Melt butter in 1 1/2 qt. saucepan. Remove from heat. Add powdered sugar and coconut. Mix well.

Shape rounded teaspoons of mixture into balls. Make an indentation in center of each, and place on plate or cookie sheet. Fill centers with the melted chocolate. Chill until firm. Store in covered container in refrigerator.

Carrot Cake

Ingredients

Submitted by Jean Higgins

Cake Mix:

1 3/4	cup sugar
2	cups flour
2	tsp. baking soda
2	tsp. cinnamon
1	tsp. salt
1	cup vegetable oil
4	eggs
3	cups finely grated carrots

Icing:

8	oz. lite cream cheese
1/4	lb. butter or margarine
1	lb. confectioner's sugar
1	cup chopped walnuts (optional)
2	tsp. vanilla

Cake Mix:

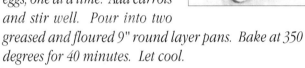

Preparation

Sift and mix dry ingredients. Add oil and stir well. Add eggs, one at a time. Add carrots and stir well. Pour into two greased and floured 9" round layer pans. Bake at 350 degrees for 40 minutes. Let cool.

Icing:

Combine cream cheese and butter; mix well. Add vanilla and sugar, and blend until smooth. Add nuts and stir. Slather on cake. Enjoy!

Raisin Scones

Ingredients

Submitted by Jean Higgins

Preheat oven to 425 degrees

2	cups flour
1/4	cup sugar
2 1/2	tsp. baking powder
1/2	cup butter
1/2	tsp. salt
1/2-1	cup raisins
2	eggs, slightly beaten
1/3	cup milk

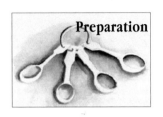

Preparation

Stir together flour, sugar, baking powder and salt. Cut in butter until size of coarse oatmeal. Add raisins, eggs, milk. Stir until just moist. Divide dough in half; shape into balls, place on <u>greased</u> cookie sheet(s). With small spatula, flatten each to 6" circle. Dip spatula in flour and score each circle into quarters (+). Bake in a preheated oven at 425 degrees for 16-18 minutes or until golden brown. Remove to rack to cool slightly. Then break each along scored lines in 4 scones.

*(It is a good idea to plump raisins before adding to mixture. Put raisins in a bowl and cover with hot or boiling water and let soak for at least 15 minutes. Drain well before mixing in with dry ingredients).

Blueberry Buckle

Submitted by Kay Horgan

Ingredients

Buckle:

3/4	cup sugar
6	Tbs. butter
1	egg
2	cups flour
1/2	tsp. salt
2	tsp. baking powder
1/2	cup milk
2	cups fresh blueberries (or frozen—if frozen, do not defrost, stir in)

Topping:

1/2	cup sugar
1/3	cup flour
1/2	tsp. cinnamon
1/4	cup soft butter

Buckle:

Preparation

Beat together sugar and butter until creamy. Add egg and beat until smooth. Stir together flour, salt and baking powder. Add to sugar, butter and egg mixture alternately with milk. Stir in blueberries. Pour into 9" square pan, greased and floured. Spread evenly. Sprinkle topping (recipe below) over evenly. Bake in 375 degree oven for 35 minutes,

Double recipe - use 9x13 pan; bake 45-50 minutes.

Cut in squares to serve

Topping:

Use pastry blender to produce crumbly, evenly moist topping.

> "No one can be wise
>
> on an empty stomach"
>
> -George Eliot

57

Tomato Lentil Soup

Submitted by Nancy Moody

Ingredients

Makes 7 1/2 cups

3	Tbs. olive oil
2	cups chopped onion
1	cup sliced celery
1/2	cup thinly sliced, quartered carrot
6	cups water
1	cup dry lentils
2/3	cup (6 oz. can) tomato paste
1/2	cup dry red wine
1/4	cup minced parsley
3	small (1/2 oz. total) vegetable bouillon cubes
1	tsp. salt
1/2	tsp. Worcestershire sauce
1/4	tsp. ground black pepper
	Shredded or grated Parmesan cheese (optional)

"Hunger is the best sauce in the world"

—Cervantes

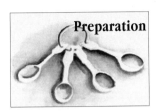

Preparation

In large Dutch oven or heavy saucepan, heat oil; sauté onion, celery and carrots until vegetables are tender. Stir in water, lentils, tomato paste, wine, parsley, bouillon cubes, salt, Worcestershire sauce, and pepper. Bring to a boil; reduce heat and simmer, uncovered, 45 to 50 minutes, or until lentils are tender. Serve with Parmesan cheese, if desired. Makes 7 1/2 cups

Curried Carrot Peanut Soup

Ingredients

Submitted by Nancy Moody

Makes 5 servings.

1	lb. carrots (about 4 large)
6	cups regular-strength chicken broth
1/2	cup finely chopped onion
1/4	cup chunky-style peanut butter
1	clove garlic, pressed or minced
2	Tbs. curry powder—to taste
1/4	cup brown rice
2	cups small broccoli flowerets

"No one can worship God
or love his neighbor
on an empty stomach."

— Woodrow Wilson

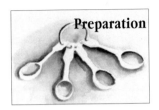

Preparation

Slice carrots; place in a 4-5 quart pan with three cups of broth. Bring to a boil and simmer until carrots are tender. Puree carrots in food processor and return to pan. Add remainder of chicken broth and remaining ingredients. Bring to a boil and simmer until rice is tender, about 30 to 40 minutes. Stir occasionally. Add broccoli and cook just until tender when pierced, about 5 minutes.

Hearty Potato Bread

Ingredients

Submitted by Nancy Moody

2	Tbs. yeast
5 1/2	cups flour (divided 2 and 3 1/2)
2	Tbs. sugar
2	tsp. salt
1 1/3	cups milk
1/2	cup butter
1 1/2	cups cooked potatoes
1	egg white
	Sesame seeds for top

"Bread is relief for all kinds of grief"

—Spanish proverb

Preparation

Mix dry yeast, 2 cups flour, sugar and salt together. Heat milk, butter and potatoes over low heat until very warm (120-130 degrees). Add liquid to dry ingredients, beat 2 minutes with mixer. Knead in remaining flour. Place in buttered bowl, cover and let rise until doubled in bulk (about 1 hour). Punch down, divide into 4 equal parts, roll each part in buttered palms to form strand about 15 inches long. Spiral wrap 2 strands together to form twist loaf, tuck ends under. Place in buttered 9x5x3-inch pan. Cover and let rise in warm place until doubled (20-30 minutes). Brush tops with egg white, sprinkle with sesame seeds. Bake at 375 degrees for 35-40 minutes.

Chickpea Soup
with Garlic and Kale

Ingredients

1	lb. chickpeas. Soak overnight in plenty of water. Rinse twice during this process.
20	cloves garlic, sliced thin
2	celery hearts, leaves and all, chopped
3	tsp. salt
	Black pepper
3	bay leaves
1 1/2	tsp. celery seed
1/3	cup extra virgin olive oil
1/2	bunch winter kale, washed, stem removed and ripped into big pieces
	Pecorino cheese, freshly grated

Preparation

In 14 cups water, put soaked chickpeas, garlic, celery, 2 tsp. of the salt, bay leaves and celery seed. Bring to a boil covered, add plenty of black pepper. Cook 1 1/2 hours and add olive oil. Continue cooking 1/2-1 hour until soup is thickened and peas are tender.

Finish seasoning to taste with salt and pepper, then add kale just to wilt.

Serve with plenty of grated cheese on top, and crusty bread. Best on the second or third day!!

East Indian Sunset Soup Bowl

Ingredients

This quick and easy one-dish meal for four to six can be simplified even further if you have leftover rice stored in your freezer. It is also easily multiplied to serve and impromptu crowd.

2	qt. chicken broth
1	tsp. turmeric
1	tsp. cumin
1	large yellow onion, sliced lengthwise in thin slices
1/4	cup minced cilantro
2	lb.boneless, skinless chicken thighs
	juice of two baby lemons
4	cups cooked Basmati rice
	Sour cream
	Fresh cilantro leaves

66

Recipe donated by Lynn Ove Mortonsen,
Author of "White Caps in the Icebox" sailing cookbook

Preparation

In a large pot, bring broth to a boil, adding turmeric, cumin, onion and minced cilantro. Trim any remaining fat from chicken and cut into bite-sized pieces. Add chicken and lemon juice to broth. Lower heat and simmer 15-20 minutes. Meanwhile, cook rice (or reheat frozen rice in microwave). Adjust the seasoning. Depending on broth used, a dash of salt may be necessary. To serve, heap piles of rice in large individual bowls. Ladle soup over rice and garnish with a dollop of sour cream and a sprinkle of fresh cilantro leaves.

"A hungry man is not a free man."

—Adlai Stevenson

Morrocan Vegetable Soup

Ingredients

Sauté mix:

4	Tbs. butter
2	yellow onions, finely chopped
4	stalks celery, finely chopped
4	large carrots, peeled, finely chopped
3	tomatoes, chopped
1	bay leaf
	Salt and pepper to taste
1	Tbs. cumin

Broth mix:

6	cups chicken broth
1	Tbs. harissa or spicy chili paste
1	cup cooked chickpeas
1	cup chopped Swiss chard or spinach

Preparation

Sauté mix:
Sauté all ingredients until soft, but do not brown

Broth mix:
Add ingredients in broth mix to the ingredients that you have sautéd . Bring all to boil, taste for additional seasonings.

Dill and Onion Bread

Ingredients

Makes one loaf

1	cup creamed cottage cheese
2	Tbs. sugar
1	Tbs. minced onion
1	Tbs. butter
2	tsp. dill seed (not weed)
1	tsp. salt
1/4	tsp. baking soda
1	egg
1	pkg. dry yeast (dissolved in 1/4 c warm water)
2 1/2	cup sifted flour

"*A loaf of bread is what we chiefly need:*
Pepper and vinegar besides
are very good indeed!"

—*Lewis Carroll,*
Through the Looking Glass

Recipe donated by Dottie Haynes,
Author of "But I Don't Want to Cook" cookbook

Preparation

Combine all the ingredients except the flour in a mixing bowl. Add the flour a little at time to form a stiff dough, beating after each addition (or if you have them, change to dough hooks on your mixer after the first addition of flour and let them do the work). Cover bowl with a wet cloth and let rise until double in size, about one hour.

Stir in the dough. Put in a well-greased 1 1/2 quart casserole dish, cover again with a redampened towel and let rise again until nearly double, approximately 40 minutes.

Bake uncovered @ 350 degrees for one hour.

Butternut and Crab Bisque

Ingredients

by Gregg Galuska
Executive Chef

1	2 1/2 to 3 pound butternut squash
1	quart chicken stock
1	large onion, diced
2	Tbs. sugar
2-3	tsp. cinnamon
1 to 2	tsp. nutmeg
2	cups heavy or whipping cream
	salt and pepper—to taste
	About 1/2 pound crabmeat
	Chopped fresh meat

"Beautiful Soup, so rich and green,

Waiting in a hot tureen!

Who for such dainties would not stoop?

Soup of the evening, beautiful soup!"

—Lewis Carroll,

Alice's Adventures in Wonderland

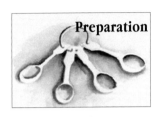

Preparation

Peel butternut squash, cut lengthwise in half, and remove seeds: dice squash into 1" pieces. In 4 quart saucepan, bring squash, chicken stock, onion, sugar, cinnamon, and nutmeg to boil. Reduce heat, cover, and simmer 20 minutes or until squash is very tender and begins to break up.

Puree squash mixture, about two cups at a time, in blender or food processor. Return squash mixture to saucepan. Add heavy cream and reheat. Stir in crab just before serving. Ladle soup into bowls and garnish with mint.

Bourbon Chocolate Pecan Cake

Ingredients

By Gregg Galuska
Executive Chef

Cake:
- 1 1/2 cups sugar
- 1 cup cocoa
- 6 eggs, lightly beaten
- 4 ounces bittersweet chocolate
- 4 ounces semisweet chocolate
- 1 cup unsalted butter
- 1/4 cup bourbon
- 1/3 cup chopped pecans
    Whipped cream (optional)
    Fresh mint leaves for garnish (optional)

Glaze:
- 4 ounces bittersweet chocolate
- 4 ounces semisweet chocolate
- 1/2 cup unsalted butter
- 1/2 cup chopped pecans

Raspberry Sauce:
- 1 cup raspberry preserves
- 1/2 cup water
- 1 Tbs. lemon juice

Cake:

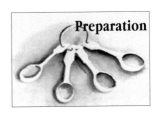

Preheat oven to 350 degrees. Sift sugar and cocoa; add eggs and mix. In a double boiler, melt chocolate and butter; add to sugar mixture. Add bourbon and pecans. Grease and line the bottom of a ten inch pan with wax paper. Pour in mixture and bake for 3/4 to one hour, until slightly soft in the center. Let cool and place upside down on a cooling rack with the pan underneath.

To serve, evenly spread glaze on top and sides of cake. Push pecans into sides and refrigerate. Once chocolate has set, cut into slices. Spoon a pool of raspberry sauce on each plate and top with cake. Serve with whipped cream and fresh mint leaves.

Glaze:

In a double boiler, melt chocolate and butter.

Raspberry Sauce

In a sauce pan, bring ingredients to a boil; simmer for 5 minutes. Strain to remove seeds and refrigerate.

Coeurs A La Creme

Ingredients

by Gregg Galuska
Executive Chef

Serves 4

This recipe calls for coeur a la creme molds, available at specialty cooking supply stores.

It must be prepared 24 hours before serving.

3/4	pint sour cream
3/4	pint cottage cheese
1/4	cup sugar
2 t	Tbs. lemon juice
1	pint raspberry puree
1/2	pint raspberries or strawberries (optional)
4	sprigs mint for garnish (optional)

"Sweet things quickly bring satiety."

—*Macro Dius*

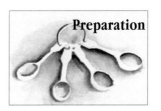

Preparation

In a mixing bowl, beat sour cream, cottage cheese, sugar, and lemon juice until smooth. Line sides of molds with slightly dampened cheese cloth or cloth napkins. Divide cheese mixture among molds and tap each gently to remove air bubbles. Wrap overhanging cloth over cheese mixture and refrigerate on a baking pan to catch excess moisture. Chill for 24 hours.

To serve, unmold hearts onto individual plates. Carefully remove cloths. Spoon raspberry puree around each heart and garnish with fresh berries and mint.

Potato Soup

Ingredients

3-4 Servings

4	large russet potatoes (peeled and cut into 1" chunks)
2	slices cooked turkey bacon
1	clove garlic (smashed and chopped)
1	medium yellow onion (chopped)
1	large carrot (chopped)
2	stalks celery (chopped)
1/2	red bell pepper (chopped)
1	bay leaf
3	dashes Tabasco® sauce
1/4	cup frozen corn
2	15 ounce cans chicken or vegetable broth
1	cup nonfat milk
1	Tbs. butter
5	Tbs. flour mixed with 1/4 cup milk (shaken until smooth)

*Place potatoes, bacon, gar-
lic, onion, carrot, celery, bell
pepper, bay leaf, Tabasco®,
corn, and broth in large heavy
bottomed sauce pan. Bring to
a boil over high heat. Reduce heat to low, cover and
cook 20 minutes. Add milk and butter - return to boil.
Thicken with flour/milk mixture by slowly pouring it
into liquid while stirring constantly. Add pepper and
parsley. Reduce heat and cook 5 minutes.
Stir yogurt in just prior to serving.*

Hot and Sour Bean Soup

Ingredients

Serves 6-8

1	lb. dry white beans
3	quarts water

(You may substitute canned, cooked beans. Be sure to wash them thoroughly to get rid of excess salt. You will need four 15 ounce cans).

3	15 ounce cans chicken or vegetable broth
1/2	medium yellow onion (chopped)
2	stalks celery (chopped)
1	red bell pepper (chopped)
1	yellow bell pepper (chopped)
1	green bell pepper (chopped)
2	gloves garlic (smashed and chopped)
1/4	cup sugar
1/2	cup white vinegar
1/4-1/2	tsp. cayenne pepper (to taste)

Recipe donated by Donald Collins
Author of "Cookbook of the Year"

Wash dry beans and soak overnight in 3 quarts water in large kettle.

Discard water in the morning and add another 3 quarts water.

Bring beans to a boil and reduce heat to low. Cook over low heat for 1 1/2 hours. Remove one cup cooked beans from kettle. Mash and set aside. Add broth, vegetables, and garlic. Bring to a boil. Reduce heat to low and cook 1/2 hour. Add sugar, vinegar and cayenne. Add mashed beans to kettle. Stir to blend thoroughly. Cover and cook another 10 minutes on low heat.

Carrot Muffins

Ingredients

Makes 12 muffins

Preheat oven to 375 degrees. Spray muffin tins with vegetable oil spray.

Dry mix:

1 1/4	cup unbleached flour
1/2	cup whole wheat flour
1/2	cup old fashioned oats
1/2	package graham crackers (crushed fine)
1/8	tsp. ginger
1/8	tsp. ground cloves
1	tsp. cinnamon
1	tsp. baking soda
2	medium or 1 large carrot (ground fine)
1/4	cup chopped walnuts
1/2	cup raisins

Wet mix:

1	egg (beaten)
1 1/4	cup milk
2	Tbs. white vinegar
3	Tbs. vegetable oil
1/3	cup molasses

Recipe donated by Donald Collins
Author of "Cookbook of the Year"

Mix the dry ingredients together in one bowl. In a separate, smaller bowl mix the wet ingredients. Stir all ingredients together (wet to dry) in large bowl and place in muffin tins.

Bake 30-35 minutes

Healthful Muffins

Ingredients

Makes 12 muffins

Preheat oven to 350 degrees

1 3/4	cup barley flour, rye flour, or unbleached white flour
1	Tbs. baking powder
1/3	cup crushed bran flakes
1/4	cup chopped walnuts
1/3	cup shredded coconut
1/2	cup smashed ripe bananas
1	cup nonfat milk with 1 tsp. vanilla added
1/4	cup unsweetened concentrated apple juice
1/2	cup cooked oats
3/4	cup chopped, dried apricots

Recipe donated by Donald Collins
Author of "Cookbook of the Year"

Mix dry ingredients in large bowl. Mix wet ingredients in another bowl and add dried apricots. Stir all ingredients together (wet to dry). Spray muffins tins with vegetable oil spray. Pour batter into tins. Bake approximately 35 minutes, or until tops are brown and spring back to the touch.

Crumb-Topped Pumpkin Custard

Ingredients

9"	pie shall unbaked
2	eggs
1 1/2	cup pumpkin
1/3	cup brown sugar
1	tsp. cinnamon
1/4	tsp. each ginger, nutmeg and salt
1	cup evaporated milk
1/4	cup water
1/3	cup orange marmalade

Topping:

1/2	cup graham cracker crumbs
1/2	cup granulated sugar
1/2	tsp. cinnamon
3	Tbs. melted butter

Preparation

Beat eggs slightly, then stir in pumpkin, brown sugar, cinnamon, ginger, nutmeg and salt. Blend in milk, water and orange marmalade. Pour into pie shell.

Bake at 350 degrees for 20 minutes. Remove and carefully sprinkle with the following topping, combined until crumbly. Bake 30 minutes longer.

" *Do as adversaries do in law,*
strive mightily,
but eat and drink as friends"

—William Shakespeare,
The Taming of the Shrew

Baked Brie Dessert

Ingredients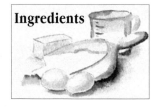

2	packages frozen puff pastry or phyllo dough
1	egg white
1	8" round of brie cheese (remove paper)

Filling:

6	oz. sundried tomatoes, pesto or low-sugar apricot jam

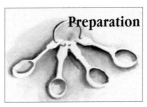
Preparation

Overlap the two sheets of dough, sealing the seams well. Brush some of the egg white over the top of dough.

Place brie in the center. If you desire a filling, make sure it is in the consistency of a paste and smooth over the top of brie, spreading evenly.

Start gathering the dough into a "ponytail" on top of the brie. Make sure the dough is tight around the cheese, but do not rip it.

Once you have the dough on top, arrange it into a pleasing design, like a flower.

HINT: Keep the dough uniform, making sure no part is heavier than the other, this helps with even baking.

Brush top with egg white to brown.

Bake on a sprayed cooking sheet for 30-40 minutes at 350 degrees. Check after 20 minutes as you do not want it to get too brown, too dry or to develop cracks.

Serve at room temperature, <u>not</u> hot.

Index of Recipe Donors

Restaurants and Caterers

ANDALUCA
Restaurant & Bar
407 Olive Way
Seattle, Washington 98101
206-382-6999

Bittersweet
211 South First Avenue
Kent, Washington 98032
206-854-0707

Bon Appetit Catering Company
Phone 206-296-6312

Cafe Flora
2901 E Madison
Seattle, Washington 98112
206-325-9100

Flying Fish Restaurant
2234 1st Avenue
Seattle, Washington 98121,
728-8595

Four Seasons Olympic Hotel
411 University Street
Seattle, Washington 98101
206-621-1700

Garden Party Flowers & Catering
206-324-1758

Hi-Spot Cafe
1410 34th Avenue
Seattle, Washington 98122
206-325-7905

Macrina Bakery and Cafe
2408 1st Avenue
Seattle, Washington 98121
206-448-4032

Marco's Supper Club
2510 1st Avenue
Seattle, Washington 98121
206-441-7801

Market Cafe at the Westin Hotel
1900 5th Avenue
Seattle, Washington 98101
728-1000

Matt's in the Market
A Seafood Bar
94 Pike Street, Suite 32 ,
Seattle, Washington 98101
206-467-7907

McCormick's Fish House & Bar
Executive Chef Gregg Galuska

Pirosmani
Georgian-Mediterranean Dining
2220 Queen Anne Ave. N,
Seattle, WA 98109,
206-285-3360

Ponti Seafood Grill
3014 3rd Avenue
Seattle, Washington 98109
206-284-3000

Space Needle Restaurant
203 6th Avenue, North
Seattle, Washington 98109
206-443-2100 or 1-800-937-9582

Virazon
329 1st Avenue
Seattle, WA 98101
233-0123

Westin Hotel
1900 5th Avenue
Seattle, Washington
206-728-1000

Authors and Chefs

Don Collins
Author of "The Cookbook of the Year"

Chef Barbara Figueroa

Dottie Haynes
Author of the "But I Don't Want to Cook" cookbook

Cori Kirkpatrick
Author of 'The Weekly Feeder" cookbook

Lynn Ove Mortensen
Author of the"White Caps in the Icebox" sailing cookbook

ORDER FORM

Qty.	Item	Price	Total
	Soupline Cookbook	$12.95	
	$3.50 for shipping and handling of first book, $2.00 to ship each additional book at the same time.		
	Washington residents please add 8.2% sales tax		
	Total enclosed		

Telephone Orders: 1-800-982-2455

Have your VISA or MasterCard ready.

Fax Orders: 1-206-281-1625

Fill out order form and fax

Postal Orders: Elliott & James Publishing
PO Box 19535
Seattle, WA 98119

Payment: Please Check One

☐ **Check**

☐ **VISA**

☐ **MasterCard**

Name: _____

Address: _____

City: _____ State: _____ Zip: _____

Credit Card: _____ Exp. Date: _____

Signature: _____

Day Time Phone: _____

Quantity discounts are available.

For more information, call 206-281-1615 ext. 207

Thank you for your order!

I understand that I may return any book for a full refund if not satisfied.

NOTES

NOTES

NOTES

NOTES

NOTES